The Woods Scientist

By Stephen R. Swinburne

With photographs by Susan C. Morse

 Houghton Mifflin Company

Boston

To my old friends Bob Cook, Øyvind Gjerde, Bill Parker, and Don Riepe,

in gratitude for all those years of great bird watching and nature study.

—S.R.S.

Text copyright © 2002 by Stephen R. Swinburne
Illustrations copyright © 2002 by Susan C. Morse
Keeping Track® is a registered trademark.

www.houghtonmifflinbooks.com

Book design by Susan Livingston
Map, p. 10, by Jerry Malone
The text of this book is set in ITC Century Book.

Library of Congress Cataloging-in-Publication Data
Swinburne, Stephen R.
The woods scientist : by Stephen R. Swinburne ;
with photographs by Susan C. Morse.
p. cm.
Summary: A devoted nature lover and animal tracker, Sue Morse shares her knowledge and love of some of the creatures that inhabit America's woodlands.
Includes bibliographical references
   ISBN 0-618-04602-X (hardcover)
   1. Forest animals—Juvenile literature. 2. Morse, Susan C.—Juvenile literature. [1. Forest animals. 2. Morse, Susan C. 3. Animal tracks. 4. Wildlife conservation.] I. Morse, Susan C. II. Title.
   QL112.S95 2002
   591.73—dc21

                                                                                          2002000302

Printed in Singapore
TWP 10 9 8 7 6 5 4

Acknowledgments

Kevin Hansen

Without the patience and commitment of Sue Morse, this book would not have gotten off the ground. I appreciated Sue's willingness to share her wild forest world with me. She never flinched under the constant barrage of questions. Thanks, Sue, for the wonderful campfire dinners and great tracking sojourns at Wolfrun.

I wish to thank Lars Botzojorns and Monica Mac in the Keeping Track office in Vermont for their support.

I also thank Kevin Hansen, Peter Lynch, William Reidig, Sean Lawson, Paul Thomas, and Tim Sullivan for their photographs of Sue.

I am grateful for my editor, Ann Rider, who lives among the deep woods of northern Minnesota within earshot of the wolf's howl, for once again lending her great care and editorial guidance to this project.

So much of creating a book requires cutting all ties and disappearing for hours into the field to do research or behind closed doors to write. For all the missed family time, I apologize to Heather, Hayley, and Devon. Your patience, love, and support keep me going.

Sue, on a mule named Bell, searches for cougar tracks in the wilds of Utah. Every year Sue takes expeditions to study mountain lions, bears, and lynx in the northern Rockies, the desert Southwest, and California.

"The Woods Were My Teacher"

"Okay, turn on your hair-covered computers," calls Sue Morse as four people gather around a small tree on a snowy November afternoon. Sue, clothed in camouflage gear, rubs her finger along the bared wood. The top and bottom of the scrape end in frayed strips of bark.

"Now, who might have made this wound and why?" she asks, turning to the group.

It is a mixed lot. A schoolteacher. A retired forester. A college student. A farmer.

"A porcupine?" offers the college student hesitantly.

"Not a bad guess," says Sue, "but porcupine tooth scars should show. Do they? Look at the tattered ends. This wound was not made by teeth."

"A moose!" says the farmer.

"You're getting warmer," says Sue. "Moose rub their antlers on trees, but they typically mark trees around four to five feet off the ground. This rub is about one and a half to two feet."

"White-tailed deer!" the schoolteacher announces.

LEFT: A buck in full velvet reclines on a late-summer day. **BELOW:** Sometimes an animal rubs so hard against a tree with its forehead and antlers that it leaves a permanent wound on the wood.

"Bingo!" says Sue. "Did the deer's horns or antlers scrape this bark?"

"Antlers," the schoolteacher answers.

"Right," says Sue. She explains that horns stay on animals for life, whereas antlers begin growing in the spring and fall off in winter. New antlers are covered in a soft tissue called "velvet." The velvet covering the antlers is so tender that deer can remove it by gently rubbing against small shrubs or trees.

Welcome to the world of Susan C. Morse. Sue is a forester, habitat ecologist, professional tracker, and passionate student of the woods. She loves solving the mystery of a claw mark on a tree or figuring out who deposited a black scat in the forest surrounding her farm. Her scientific method is simple and neat. She calls it

Deer Rubs

White-tailed deer mate throughout late October, November, and early December in the northern forests. During the rut, or mating season, bucks rub and thrash small trees, often leaving the trees shredded and torn. People believe that deer do this to remove their velvet, but research has revealed the key reason. Scientists believe that bucks rub trees to send a message about their social and sexual status. Bucks may signal, for example, how ready they are to mate or what standing they hold in the herd. "Rubs serve as bulletin boards in the forests that other deer see and smell," says Sue. "Not only does the shredded and exposed sapwood serve as a visual signpost, but deer rub scent from glands located on their foreheads and in the corners of their eyes onto the wounded surface of the tree. The secretions left on the tree communicate a message that other deer can smell." While female deer rub trees too, the bucks do the most rubbing during fall. On average, bucks rub trees that are one to four inches in diameter; big, mature deer may make huge rubs on trees of six to twelve inches in diameter.

"ground truthing." She learns the facts by walking in the forest and making observations, much as naturalists John Burroughs and Henry David Thoreau and scientist Jane Goodall did in decades past.

Sue is at home in the forest. She's read woods ever since she could remember. She believes that by reading the forests she can help save them.

Sue Morse grew up in the forests and farming country of Mount Airy and Norristown, Pennsylvania. Her playground was the Wissahickon woods, as well as her grandfather's 2,490-acre farm and tree nursery. She comes from a long line of landscapers and foresters, and her parents, grandfather, and great-grandfather all planted and grew trees for a living. Sue is a fourth-generation forester. She likes to say, "Forestry runs in my sap." Sue tends an arboretum that she has planted over the past twenty-six years. This collection of trees features more than 100 species, or varieties, of conifers from all over the world.

Sue's grandfather, Norman Morse, used his team of draft horses to pull a huge tree to plant in another location. "My grandfather gave me some good advice," says Sue. "He said, 'Be content to learn one thing every week—something about one bird, a plant, a mineral, the track of an animal, and think how much you'll know in ten, twenty, or thirty years.'"

"We weren't the sort of family that watched a lot of TV," says Sue. "Our parents filled our lives with a love of animals and the outdoors. My grandfather was my hero. I remember him sticking sunflower seeds in his big, hairy ears for his chickadee friends, whom he called 'Chick' and 'A'Dee.' The small birds would fly over and pluck out the seeds and eat them, much to the delight of all of us.

"My grandfather gave me rocks and minerals for Christmas and birthdays," continues Sue. "And I had every pet I

Sue Morse scans her beloved Vermont forest.

wanted, provided I took care of it! Horses, snakes, mice, rabbits, dogs, cats."

Sue describes herself as a "catoholic." Her lifelong love of cats started with her beloved housecats.

"Other girls were given dolls for Christmas, but my parents knew I only wanted stuffed animals, especially big cats," remembers Sue. Tuffy, her Siberian tiger, was always her favorite.

Sue has loved forests all her life. When she was in high school, her parents divorced and Sue's mother remarried and moved the family to the suburbs of Philadelphia. Every day after school Sue ran more than four and a half miles to the Wissahickon woods. That passion to get to the woods turned her into a strong distance runner. In 1967, as a senior in high school, Sue became the first woman in the United States to run a twenty-six-mile marathon. She still runs four times a week along the logging roads near her northern Vermont farm.

"Next to the woods," says Sue, "books were my greatest teachers. By the time I was in high school, Rachel Carson and her very important book *Silent Spring* profoundly moved me."

The woods of Sue Morse's childhood in southeastern Pennsylvania have changed. Wildlife habitat has shrunk or disappeared altogether. Housing developments, strip malls, and corporate offices have sprung up like mushrooms on a wet spring morning. And what were once miles and miles of undisturbed forests have become a patchwork of suburban woodlots crisscrossed by highways. Wildlife squeezes into smaller and smaller home territories. It's not just this loss of wild land that worries Sue, but more specifically the slicing of the remaining natural habitat.

"We need to preserve large chunks of wild habitat—thousands of acres or even hundreds and hundreds of square miles—'core habitats,' as we call them," says Sue. "We also need to keep those rich core habitats linked together. Only then can we protect the planet's rich biodiversity." Sue explains that the land connecting one wild habitat with another is called a "corridor" or "linkage zone."

She thinks a lot about wildlife corridors these days.

Biodiversity, Sue says, is "nature's dynamic interplay." Imagine the forest as a huge puzzle in motion, and the variety of living things—trees, shrubs, flowers, mushrooms, mammals, birds, reptiles, amphibians, fish, and insects—as moving pieces in that puzzle. And imagine this great puzzle of plants and animals, hundreds, even thousands of different species, dependent on one another, living together in sun and rain, throughout winter, spring, summer, and fall. Now imagine removing a piece of the puzzle—say, an insect or bird: the puzzle loses its strength. Kill off enough pieces, or species, and the puzzle falls apart. Every living thing counts.

The remaining protected forests in the lower 48 states are home to more than 3,000 species of animals and 10,000 species of plants, including 260 threatened or endangered species of animals and plants.

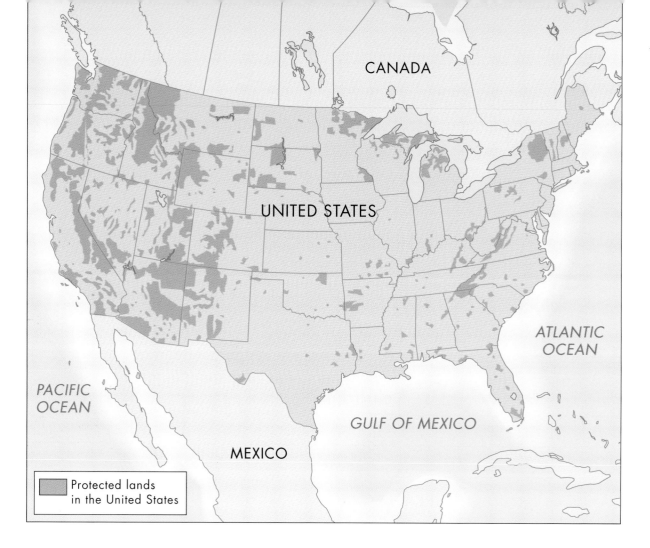

Protected lands
in the United States

CANADA

UNITED STATES

PACIFIC
OCEAN

ATLANTIC
OCEAN

GULF OF MEXICO

MEXICO

All of earth, scientists estimate, is home to 14 million species of plants and animals—and only 1.75 million have been documented. Harvard biologist E. O. Wilson states that we are losing species at a rate not seen since the dinosaurs disappeared 65 million years ago. Wilson estimates that this current rate of extinction is 10,000 times faster than what's "normal" or natural. He projects that within the next twenty-five years, one of every five species could die out unless we do our part to save their habitat.

In the face of so much habitat loss, Sue worries about keeping wildlands whole and connected so animals can come and go. Scientists call animals that are most vulnerable to habitat fragmentation "indicator species." Grizzly bears, river otters, wolverines, Canada lynxes and bobcats, and other forest carnivores are examples of indicator species. The presence of these animals in the woods is an indicator of a healthy habitat. The decline or absence of such creatures may serve as a warning. Their decline may indicate an unhealthy habitat, with too many prey and not enough predators—a landscape stripped of its animal and plant diversity.

Unlike birds, which fly to a new home, large mammals such as grizzly bears,

In 1803, when Lewis and Clark explored the western United States, about 100,000 grizzly bears lived between the Mississippi River and the Pacific Ocean. Today, fewer than 1,000 grizzlies can be found in the contiguous 48 states. The loss of forest habitat from development, roads, mining, and irresponsible logging threatens the survival of grizzly bears. In these states, the grizzly bear is an endangered species. If the population of these great bears gets too low, the species could approach the brink of extinction.

Keeping Track volunteers doing a track count. There are many Keeping Track success stories. For example, a group called the Piscataquog Watershed Association in southern New Hampshire worked with Keeping Track to identify an important bobcat area. Through habitat monitoring, the group stopped a proposed snowmobile trail and moved the site of a proposed town dump. This was easier than forcing the resident bobcats to relocate and find suitable habitat. All in all, 1,500 acres have now been set aside for bobcats and other wildlife.

wolves, and mountain lions expand into new territory by walking. A four-lane highway or other development is often a roadblock to traveling wildlife. Animals living in fragmented habitats are cut off from other members of their species. They may not be able to find adequate food and cover or reproduce and have their young find home ranges of their own.

"Even the biggest parks in the country," says Sue, "such as two-million-acre Yellowstone National Park and six-million-acre Adirondack Park, need to be connected to other big tracts of lands so wild animals may naturally move back and forth.

"Over the next few decades as human population increases, without doubt, the number-one conservation concern," warns Sue, "will be the preservation of habitat and keeping wild habitats connected with other wild habitats."

Sue Morse has never been one to talk about an environmental problem without trying to find a solution. In 1994, she formed a nonprofit conservation organization called Keeping Track. Its mission is to inspire community participation in the long-term stewardship of wildlife habitat. Sue believes that one of the best ways to conserve habitat is to learn about the habitat in your own community. Keeping Track teaches concerned adults and children to observe, interpret, and record evidence of wildlife in their region. Wild habitat has a much better chance of staying wild under the watchful eyes of a whole community of knowledgeable and dedicated wildlife enthusiasts.

"Recording evidence of wildlife tracks and signs will not give you an

BELOW: Bobcat tracks. **LEFT:** Bobcat looking down on game trail from ledge. "By knowing how to 'read' tracks and signs," says Sue, "we can make a better case for wildlife in our communities and positively influence plans for development, roads, recreation, industry, and ski areas. All of a sudden our animal neighbors won't be invisible creatures we've seen only on TV. They'll be real wildlife in need of real habitat."

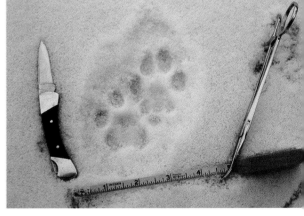

accurate estimate of how many bears or mountain lions are out there," says Sue, "but track counts will tell us who's in the neighborhood—what wildlife is present. Over years of time, with many data being collected and interpreted, we will learn the whereabouts of critical habitats such as denning areas and travel corridors. Also, if you're walking in the forest and you can identify the track in the snow as that of a bobcat, you feel connected to this elusive wild neighbor and to the vital habitat that she or he requires."

Habitat protection will secure a future for the black bear.

The Bear Went over the Mountain

or close to thirty years Sue's home base has been a farm tucked at the end of a dirt road among 200 square miles of wild country in northern Vermont. She calls her place and surrounding wild lands Wolfrun. Sue has studied the mountain lion in Arizona, the northern Rockies, California, and Alberta, Canada. She's searched for ocelot and jaguar in Mexico and tracked the elusive lynx in Maine, Montana, and Canada. No matter how far Sue travels in search of wild carnivores, her home is Wolfrun, nestled on the edge of a mixed hardwood and coniferous forest. Her small cabin, crammed with a lifetime's collection of thousands of books, is also her office. Outside her door, within this rich and extensive forest, lies her laboratory. And it is here she has dedicated her life to saving the woods by teaching people about them.

"Just like we need water, food, a home, a place to recreate and grow, so does the bear that climbed this tree," says Sue. We had hiked less than a mile into the forest behind her farm on a crisp October afternoon.

Sue works every day to save habitat for creatures that live in wild landscapes like Vermont's northern Green Mountains. "At the current rate of land development in the U.S.," she says, "we'll lose 15 million acres of wildlife habitat in five years."

15

Stephen R. Swinburne

Stephen R. Swinburne

ABOVE: Claw marks of black bear on beech tree. **BELOW:** Leaves of beech tree. "Beechnuts are the most important food supply for bears up here in the northern forest," Sue says. "Bears are excellent climbers and plunk themselves in the canopy and break off branches to get at the nuts. They may eat fifty to several hundred beechnuts in a sitting."

We crane our necks skyward and follow sets of claw marks up the smooth, gray trunk of a towering beech tree.

We haven't walked very far from the beech tree when Sue points out a half dozen black lumps of bear scat among the leaf litter. It's filled with bits of beechnuts.

"A bear memento," says Sue, smiling.

Sue explains that we practice "safe scat" at Keeping Track: "We never touch animal feces with our bare hands or bring them close to our faces. Scat can be dangerous. Some raccoon scat, for example, harbors eggs of a roundworm parasite that could make you very sick. It's fun to examine animal scat, but use the chopstick method. Use two small sticks or branches to handle the scat instead of your fingers."

Seed Dispersal

Sue has learned that bears and the other carnivores she studies are great dispersers of plants. "Bears, coyotes, fishers, and foxes are all carrying in their colons the seeds from a variety of fruits that they've eaten," says Sue. "Even the strictest carnivore, like the bobcat, which usually does not eat fruit or plants at all, is carrying in its own colon the seeds eaten by the prey animal that it then ate." She's found that these seeds pass through the digestive system and are unharmed. In fact, many of these seeds are prepared for germination by the stomach acids of the carnivore and eventually grow into more plants.

"Mammals like a bobcat or a bear or a mountain lion have a tremendous role to play in life," says Sue. "I call this 'biodiversity at work.' A wide-ranging animal eats a seed on one mountain range and defecates on another. They are dispersing the very plants they need to survive; they are literally giving these seeds a ride."

ABOVE: A black bear eating common juniper fruit. **LEFT:** Bear turd full of serviceberry seeds. **RIGHT:** Seeds that germinated in bear turd. "When in doubt, follow it out. Don't be a nerd, find that turd!" Sue once conducted an experiment comparing the germination rate of seeds found in bear and coyote scat with the seeds she collected from the plant. With those she collected, Sue artificially prepared the seeds for germination by soaking them in water, storing them in the cold for two months (to mimic the effects of winter), and then putting them in a blender for a couple of seconds (to mimic the effects of time and wear). She made a remarkable discovery—those seeds found in bear and coyote scat had a much higher germination rate.

This mountainside in Vermont's Green Mountains is not the only place the bear needs. A female bear may need a home range of ten to twenty square miles, and a male may need twenty to thirty square miles. The size of the home range depends on the quality or "productivity" of the habitat. Productivity means the abundance and diversity of food bears must have, such as berries and nuts from cherry, beech, and oak trees. "If our tracking data show that an area is a core habitat for bear, bobcat, fisher, mink, wolverine, lynx, otter, and other animals," says Sue, "it's a very special area. Such plant and animal biodiversity deserves protection. Subdivisions with still more houses, shopping malls, and roads are not always the best choices."

We move on, clomping through the autumn forest, making as little noise as possible but still sounding like a gang of rooting pigs. It seems as if every leaf in Vermont is underfoot. Small branches snap and crack. "Of course, every animal in earshot of us is in hiding or long gone," Sue reminds us. "But our purpose in tracking is not to see the animal but to learn about each species and its place in the environment." We slog up a rise and stand on top of a knoll with widely spaced oak, beech, hemlock, cherry, and maple and abundant woody shrubs. A walk in the forests with Sue Morse is mind-boggling. It's impossible to absorb all of the wood lore that pours from her.

"This is great bear country," Sue announces, beaming with a look that says there's no other place she'd rather be. With a sweeping motion of her arm, Sue points to the broad, expansive view of the green summits to the hardwood ridges and adjacent foothills, to the wetlands and valleys below. She then asks us to ponder a question: "*How* can we make sure that this landscape stays this way?"

Two ravens fly above the forest canopy. Those ravens have about an hour's flight to shopping malls, gas stations, and traffic jams in Burlington, the largest city in Vermont. Sue worries about encroaching development.

"Think about it: In 1900, the population of the earth was 2 billion," says Sue. "In 2000, the population was 6 billion. In 2050, more than 10 billion people may live on Earth. We are standing in a place within a day's drive of 60 million people. Billions of people contribute to ecological destruction such as global warming and acid rain, both lethal dangers to life on earth. Our use of polluting cars has more than doubled in the past twenty years.

"For our good, for the sake of wildlife, for the wondrous variety of all life on the planet, *can* we agree to limit ourselves? The conservation of all of these animals depends upon our willingness to make sacrifices. If a dirt road is paved, how long before the road gets widened and new homes, 'starter castles,' poke out of the tree line?

"Where do you suppose the bears that use this vast forested region are right now?" Sue asks us. "They're working the other side of this ridge for acorns and beechnuts. Come winter, they'll den up near the top of that mountain across the valley. In spring, they'll head for the wetlands down the valley to search for early spring greens. Bears and bobcats require large home ranges. Can you see why a protected patch of woods here and a protected mountainside there do not secure their future, much less the future of their offspring?"

Sue climbed this black cherry tree to inspect a "bear nest." These big clumps of broken branches high in a tree's crown do not show where a bear has slept but where a bear has eaten. Bears climb into the crowns of black cherry, wild apple, oak, and especially American beech and sit in one spot while bending and breaking branches to dine on the energy-rich fruits and nuts.

Paul Thomas

ABOVE: A black bear marking white birch tree. **RIGHT:** Bear claw marks.

We follow Sue into a stand of trees. She stops short at one of them.

"Cool as a moose! What's this?" she says, running one hand across the face of the bark. Sue shows us claw marks, three to five inches long, almost lost in the rough texture of the bark.

"Hey, it's where a bobcat clawed!" shouts a young boy.

"Are you sure?" asks Sue. "They're awfully long for a cat. And these scratches are five feet off the ground. A bobcat would need stilts to get that high."

"Looks like bear to me," says a retired boat captain, fingering the marks with his outstretched hand.

Stephen R. Swinburne

"Okay, good," says Sue. "You're right. These are black bear claw marks, but what about these two holes?"

Sue points to the two mysterious, half-inch-deep holes in the bark, just below the claw marks.

"Now, who would have made these?" she asks.

"They look like someone hammered nails and then removed them," says one student.

"They're not nail holes," says Sue.

"Woodpecker!" call two sixth-grade girls.

LEFT: A black bear rubs its back against an evergreen tree. BELOW: A young girl looks at black bear hair left on an evergreen. "Half of tracking is knowing where to look," says Sue. "The other half is looking."

"Good guess, but another animal did this," Sue tells us. She is patient, prompting us and encouraging us to really open our eyes and look.

"Squirrel?" says the boy.

"Bug holes?" says the captain.

"Fungus?" shouts another.

"Okay, okay," calls Sue. "All good guesses, but I can see you're as stumped as I was when I first saw this on a tree. Here's how I figured it out."

Sue reaches down and opens her backpack. She hauls out a lump wrapped in an orange wool stocking cap. She peels away the cap.

Sue inspects teeth and claw marks. She puts a stick in either side of a bite mark to show where the bear's upper and lower canine teeth came together.

Sue sometimes likes to "become" a bear. She rakes the trunk with her hands and presses her face to the tree to bite the bark. Finally, she turns and leans her back against the tree, rubbing her shoulders and the back of her neck. Sue interprets: "A bear stood on its hind legs and raked this white birch with its claws. You can see these four long scratches. Here, close to the claw marks, the bear bit the tree. It then pressed its body against the bark and rubbed vigorously. Look here." Sue holds a white index card to the tree bark so the dark hairs that came off the bear show up clearly against the background of the card.

"Meet Yorick," says Sue, holding up the bleached white skull of a black bear. "Alas, poor Yorick taught me how to make sense of these two mystery holes. The claw marks were obvious, but it was Yorick who helped me figure out that these two holes were bear bite marks."

Everyone claps. Yorick takes a bow. We walk on, smiling, aware that the forest around us is more alive than ever.

Stephen R. Swinburne

Stephen R. Swinburne

Sue pries open Yorick's jaws, tilts the skull sideways, and fits the bear's upper and lower canine teeth perfectly into the holes on the bark.

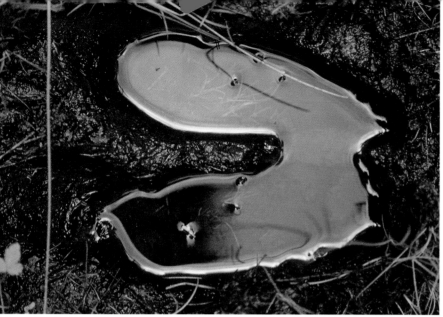

A moose track

Don't Build and They Will Come

We're standing on the edge of a forest marsh on a sunny day when Sue runs over to a nearby pile of droppings. She plunks herself down and begins to eat them.

"Wow, delicious!" Sue grins between bites. "Moose turds are great!"

All eyes bulge wide open. Mouths hang slack. We know Sue is into the woods, but tasting animal droppings? When she can't hold it in any longer, Sue pulls open her jacket and digs out a plastic bag full of large chocolate malted balls.

"Anyone care for a moose marble?" says Sue with a devilish smile, holding out her bag.

"In 1978, on a late winter walk, I came across moose-barking on a tree," says Sue, "and nearby I found a grand pile of moose pellets. It was so exciting to see evidence of an animal that I'd never seen here before. We had moose at Wolfrun!"

Sue tells us that other than rubs, scat, and tracks, another sign in the forests is "barked" trees. The bark of these trees has been stripped off and eaten. In the Northeast, white-tailed deer usually bark hemlock trees, whereas moose strip bark from maples. In the Rockies, moose bark aspen trees; in Alaska, they bark willows. Deer and moose, as members of the deer family, have incisor teeth on only their lower jaws, so barking is done in an upward direction, leaving long, tooth-shaped gouges. Sue's hypothesis is that moose and deer—both herbivores—bark trees to eat essential minerals found within the sapwood. These minerals help all moose build strong skeletons, help cow, or female, moose make milk for their young, and help bull, or male, moose grow big antlers. Moose barking generally doesn't kill the tree unless the moose completely girdles it. Girdling is

Trackers investigating moose-barked tree.

Motorists need to be cautious at moose-crossing signs. "I love moose," says Sue, "but we have over 50,000 of them in the northeastern region. Without the healthy influence of predation, including wolves, cougars, and human hunters to help control the population, an overpopulation of moose could lead to a number of problems, including car accidents and habitat deterioration. Think about it—moose can eat twenty-five to forty pounds of plants a day!"

the removal of the complete ring of bark. Girdling usually kills the tree because it interrupts the flow of nutrients from the leaves to the roots.

During the 1800s, most of Vermont's and New Hampshire's mature forest was logged or cleared for livestock. With their habitat gone, the moose, native animals of New England, died off. Moose populations began growing again in the early 1900s for two main reasons: the forest was growing back and beavers were once again creating more wetlands and ponds. Aquatic vegetation such as pond weeds and lilies provides important nutrition to moose in spring and summer. From a couple of dozen moose in the 1940s, Vermont now has more than 4,000 moose. An estimated 2,000 moose lived in Maine at the turn of the century; now some 35,000 moose are known to live there.

There are no natural predators, such as wolves and cougars, to stop the moose population from growing quickly. But that could be changing. Could the northeastern United States once again be home to packs of wild wolves? Many people think it could. Northern New England still contains millions of acres of wild lands—suitable wolf habitat. Ontario and Quebec, across the United States border in Canada, support large populations of wolves. Wolves might travel from Canada and disperse into Maine and from there throughout the region. If they did, they would find plenty of prey—moose, deer, beaver. The howl of the wolf has not been heard in the Northeast for more than 100 years. But wildlife biologists estimate that many thousands of wolves could one day live there.

"The wolf will come back," says Sue, "if we let it. The habitat wolves need and the corridors that connect them already exist. If we can preserve this wild land, I predict the wolf will return to the northern forest in our lifetime. Wolves are very adaptable. It's just a matter of time before it happens."

In her lifetime, Sue has witnessed the return of moose, beaver, turkey, and gray squirrel to the forested habitats of Wolfrun. While she is happy about these animals expanding their range, she worries about the future of more wide-ranging carnivores, like mountain lions, black bears, and wolves.

Animal species such as lions, bears, and wolves have been on the earth for a

Moose and calf. Many biologists believe the moose population in the northern forest is growing by 10 to 15 percent a year. If that's true, with 50,000 moose present in the forest today, consider how many moose the northern forest will have in twenty years.

Keeping Track volunteers call a moose. Sue often imitates the sound of animals. "In order to get closer to a bull moose," she says, "I imitate the call of the cow moose, which sounds like a nasal, whining moan. If I want to sound like the bull, I make the 'plunge grunt.' It's like a rock plunging into a pool followed by a grunt."

very long time. For example, scientists believe the wolf, whose scientific name is *Canis lupus*, evolved from a primitive group of meat-eaters called creodonts. Creodonts roamed the earth 100 to 120 million years ago. Black bears came to North America from Asia 500,000 years ago. The Asian lynx arrived here 20,000 years ago.

The evolution of early humans began on the plains of Africa only 5 million years ago. Wolves, cats, and bears were here on Earth long before we appeared. "How would we feel if such ancient species perished?" asks Sue.

"Black bear and bobcat populations may be doing very well at present throughout the United States," she continues, "but what about 50 or 100 years

The gray wolf is a threatened species in the U.S. Biologists estimate there may be approximately 500 wolves in northwestern Montana, central Idaho, and the Yellowstone area. Some of these wolves were part of the U.S. Fish and Wildlife Service Wolf Reintroduction Program. There are also small populations of gray wolves living in northeastern Minnesota, northern Wisconsin, and Michigan's Upper Peninsula.

RIGHT: A cougar and its prey, a white-tailed deer. **BELOW:** Deer hair in a cougar track. Scientists know that wolves and lions keep ungulate populations in check. Without predators, huge numbers of elk, moose, and deer would get out of control, eating so many plants that other wildlife, including amphibians, birds, and insects, could not survive.

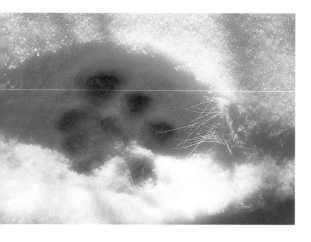

from now? Will the core habitats and corridors still support these animals? And are people ready to share habitat with wolves, mountain lions, grizzlies, and wolverines in the wild forests of their states?

"Some people might ask why it's important for forests to have wolves and lions," says Sue. "But scientists know that predators play a big role in nature. And we are the stewards of this planet. We have both a moral and a practical responsibility to safeguard the diversity of life."

"Although nearly 80 percent of northern New England and northern New York is covered in forest," Sue explains, "human population growth could threaten this land as future habitat for carnivores such as lynx, bobcats, bear, and wolf." Wolves alone need lots of wilderness to survive. Researchers in Alaska discovered that a wolf pack of ten used a home range of 5,000 square miles in winter.

The steep, ledgy landscape of Cougar Knob is a perfect habitat for bobcats. They use these cliff faces as places to hide, to raise kittens, and to sun themselves in the winter. Sue calls them "bobby perches." A bobcat's chances of survival are improved if these rocky ledges and cliffs are protected.

Keeping Forests Wild

Stephen R. Swinburne

Out of respect for the forest creatures giving birth and raising young, Sue rarely goes into the woods in late April, May, and early June. But on an unusually cold and blustery Mother's Day several years ago, with a couple of inches of fresh, wet snow on the ground in northern Vermont, Sue had the most remarkable experience of her tracking career. She never saw the animal but read its sign in the snow.

"A lot of people were furious at such weather in May, but I was thrilled," says Sue. "I took advantage of the snow cover to check animal tracks near Cougar Knob, one of the remote habitats in the mountains near Wolfrun."

At the base of a large broken cliff face, Sue soon found sign of Bobette, a female bobcat that she had been tracking for a number of years. Sue has seen and measured the tracks of this particular bobcat so many times she knows them by heart.

"It was obvious to me that Bobette was denning somewhere near Cougar Knob," she tells us. "I show a lot of respect for all the creatures that I'm studying and never try to get too close or pinpoint exactly where they are denning or hiding. Just like we wouldn't want to wake up in the middle of the night and find some

Sue tracking a fisher. She always backtracks the animal rather than tracking forward. Following right behind a bobcat or fisher, for example, especially in winter, can frighten the animal and thereby deplete its precious energy supply and lessen its ability to survive. Backtracking follows the tracks of where the animal has been, not where it's going.

33

A bobcat is secure on a rocky ledge or "escape habitat," as Sue calls it.

stranger in our bedroom, I don't invade an animal's home. We're just guests out there. They *live* there."

On that day, Sue tells us, she discovered a curious sequence of multiple bobcat tracks. She then found sign of the bobcat making the same exact journey three different times. "I found where Bobette jumped down from ledge to ledge and walked down secret little cliff edges," says Sue. "And then she made perfect precision jumps through open space, landing on small, secluded knobs without slipping or falling or missing. Eventually she moved out of this one rocky, cliffy area to another rocky place several hundred feet away. Then she reversed the journey, traversing the same difficult route—jumping from perch to perch and walking along six-inch ledges until she got to where she was going and to where, of course, I never went, out of respect for her.

"I was bursting with excitement. I had to force myself to quietly study the sign lest I shout for joy and possibly disturb Bobette.

"It soon became obvious to me that what she was doing was moving her kittens from one location to another. I had tears in my eyes when I finally put all that together; she was making those identical trips, each time with a bobcat kitten in her mouth!"

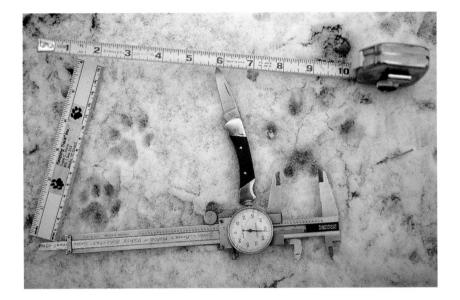 

ABOVE LEFT: Bobcat tracks, left, next to lynx track, right. **ABOVE RIGHT:** Bobcat kitten at den site on ledge. "Thirty-plus years of studying and trailing northwoods bobcats," says Sue, "have taught me that without doubt their four most important behaviors are sleeping, resting, dozing, and napping. Just as your housecat will move from a once sunny windowsill to a plush chair by the woodstove, bobcats spend a great deal of time resting in comfortable places—places that afford them warmth and security, especially in winter. The perfect bobcat place is a rocky, secluded ledge facing the sun, steep enough to keep kittens safe from hungry coyotes and other predators."

"If your eyes are in front—you hunt. If your eyes are to the side—you'd better hide," says Sue. "The forward-facing eyes of the lynx, **RIGHT,** help it to judge distances accurately. This is important when paws are your only weapons and dinner is a moving target." Eyes on the side, like the snowshoe hare's, **BELOW,** give the animal a wider view of its surroundings, allowing it to better see what might be sneaking up.

What I've Learned About the Lynx

"As a tracker," says Sue, "I've found it very useful to look at the feet of the animal I'm tracking, or even to just study my housecat's feet or my dog's. You can learn a lot about what you expect to see in tracks just by looking at feet."

Lynx—their tracks and feet—fascinate Sue, and several times she has had the opportunity to study lynx feet up close. For thousands of years, this wild cat has lived among the deep snows of the northeastern United States, the Rocky Mountains, Canada, and Alaska. Their large, furry paws have evolved into perfect snowshoes. Lynx feet have twice the surface area of the feet of their similar-sized cousin, the bobcat. With big feet and long legs, lynx are perfectly adapted to chasing and capturing snowshoe hare.

"Lynx have very distinctive tracks in the snow," Sue says. "Every winter I track lynx to try to learn more about this amazing creature."

She discovered something about lynx that was not documented in the scientific literature before. After studying nearly 100 sets of tracks, as well as skinning the feet of five deceased lynx, Sue found that the lynx's hind feet are slightly larger than its front feet when the hind feet toes are spread apart. She believes that this unique physical feature contributes to the lynx's awesome ability to leap and switch direction with incredible speed and precision when chasing a hare in deep snow.

"The more specialized an animal becomes," says Sue, "the more specialized its whole body must become in order to do what it must do to live." Unlike the coyote, a generalist that will hunt and eat whatever is available, the lynx is a specialist, hunting and eating mainly snowshoe hare.

She believes that just by making simple observations about an animal—in this case, the lynx's feet—you can discover new information. "The neat thing about natural science," she says, "is that there is a lot of information we don't have. A world of discovery awaits young naturalists."

The lynx is now listed as a threatened species in the lower forty-eight states. Bobcats, **ABOVE,** are not currently threatened or endangered. But as the valley habitats throughout the United States fill with development, bobcats may become at risk too. Unlike lynx, which have large furry feet to survive in snow-filled northern forests, bobcats need to retreat to the lower valley and foothill habitats in winter and may face starvation if too much of their habitat is destroyed.

ABOVE: River otter. **RIGHT:** River otter slides. In addition to reading tracks, rubs, and scat, Sue loves seeing signs of animals at play, including otters belly-sliding on pond ice.

Timothy J. Sullivan

Sue and a friend setting up a remote camera in the woods at Wolfrun. What Sue has learned through her years of tracking has led her to suspect that there are four bobcats living at Wolfrun. But perhaps there are more. In the next five years, she plans to conduct research using remote cameras and video footage to visually identify the bobcats whose tracks she's found. "This will correlate my track count data with camera capture data," she explains.

On Sue's mountain at Wolfrun, there are no trails. She probably wouldn't use them if there were. Sue sometimes picks up game trails, vague paths that deer and other wildlife use, but mostly it's bushwhacking. She's studied these forests for nearly thirty years. She knows where the bobcats rest on sunny ledges, where the moose give birth to calves by the wetlands in spring, where sows and bear cubs gorge on beechnuts in the late summer, where the otters slide on the ice in winter. As much as she loves this forest and knows about its animals, Sue also knows she has so much more to learn.

"Newt alert! Newt alert!" Sue calls out to the small group of students she is

ABOVE: The eastern newt is an amphibian that starts life in spring as an egg in a pond or quiet stream. A larva hatches from the egg in late spring and by late summer is transformed into a young newt, called a red eft. The eft leaves the water and spends one to three years on land, where it eats small worms and insects. When mature, efts change from red to greenish brown, return to water to breed, and remain there for the rest of their lives. **RIGHT:** White-tailed deer. "Woodland animals basically need the same things we need," says Sue, "water, food, and cover."

leading. She asks the person behind her to pass the word back to watch out for the animal underfoot. A red eft lumbers like a Day-Glo miniature dinosaur across our path.

Sue has organized like-minded neighbors and local and state officials in forming the Chittenden County Uplands Project. The goal of the project is to preserve the natural landscape of the area, one of the wildest regions in Vermont. She is passionate about saving the rich biodiversity of this 200-square-mile area of mountain, forest, and wetland habitat.

"No matter how huge this project seems to be, no matter how daunting a task," Sue affirms, "I've decided I'm going to dedicate my life to saving wild forests. No great thing has been done by a human on this planet, no great project has ever been accomplished, without some individual or group of individuals starting it somewhere and keeping at it until the job got done."

A swamp in Vermont's Chittenden County Uplands area.

"We need to keep the forests wild," says Sue. "We need to keep the deserts wild and the tropical forests wild and the canyons wild and the oceans wild and the Arctic tundra wild. And we need to keep these regions biologically connected to one another. . . . A large part of keeping forests wild is learning to draw boundaries between where humans should be and where we should stay out."

41

An "Alligator Alley" in Florida is investigated by a tracker.

Sue challenges you to tackle some of these projects.

What are some ways we can redesign highways so bears, bobcats, cougars, and other wildlife can safely cross roads? Build a model highway that shows how animals might use underpasses, overpasses, and other wildlife crossings. Try contacting the Florida Department of Transportation to find out more about the "Alligator Alley" underpasses, which have allowed safe passage of a wide variety of creatures, from alligators and armadillos to Florida's endangered panther.

What kind of art project could you make in school to explain what wildlife corridors are or to show the effects of habitat fragmentation?

Sue suspects moose and deer bark trees to eat essential minerals (calcium, potassium, phosphorus) in the sap that have been lost during lactation and production of antlers. *Can you design an experiment that proves that these minerals are more available in the trees that these ungulates choose than in the trees that are largely untouched?*

How can we interpret the messages deer are sending in the chemical secretions left when they rub on trees?

While many projects have been done using radio collars on wild animals, there's still so much more to learn about elusive carnivores such as grizzly and black bears, mountain lions, lynx, and otters. *Can you research some of the findings scientists have made using radio collars on animals?*

Can you discover which animals are living in your area?

Helping the Forests Stay Wild

• In the wilderness, learn to leave cars, snowmobiles, dirt bikes, ATVs, and other motorized conveniences behind. Take only photographs; leave only footprints.

• Housecats kill millions of songbirds every year. Keep your cat inside during nesting season (spring and summer). If your cat must be outside, put a bell on its collar.

• Think local. Is there a wildlife habitat in your town or area that needs protection?

• Plant a tree.

• Help your parents, school, Boy Scout or Girl Scout troops, or other organizations form a Keeping Track program. Get involved in habitat protection.

ABOVE: Panther-crossing sign in Florida. Many biologists believe that southern Florida's ecosystem is the most endangered in the country due to population growth, farming, and urban development. It's estimated that fewer than fifty critically endangered Florida panthers exist today.
LEFT: A panther track in Florida mud.

Stephen R. Swinburne

If you are interested in learning more about Keeping Track and the Keeping Track Youth Program, please write to Keeping Track, Inc., P.O. Box 444, Huntington, Vermont 05462, or visit its Web site at www.keepingtrackinc.org.

ABOVE: Sue and Los Penasquitos Canyon Preserve volunteers in San Diego, California, look at bobcat tracks going under a very busy freeway through a culvert. Concerned about the loss of biodiversity in this preserve, Keeping Track helped set up a monitoring program enabling trained volunteers to track local wildlife, including bobcats, coyotes, deer, weasels, and even the occasional cougar in San Diego's outlying rural habitats.

For more information, contact

The Wildlands Project
P.O. Box 455
Richmond, Vermont 05477
www.wild-earth.org

Sky Island Alliance
738 N. 5th Avenue
Suite 201
Tucson, Arizona 85705
www.skyislandalliance.org

The Nature Conservancy
4245 N. Fairfax Drive
Suite 100
Arlington, Virginia 22203
www.nature.org

The Wildlife Conservation Society
North America Program
2300 Southern Boulevard
Bronx, New York 10460
www.wcs.org

The National Wildlife Federation
11100 Wildlife Center Drive
Reston, Virginia 20190-5362
www.nwf.org

Check out local land trusts and state wildlife departments. These organizations are working hard to conserve wildlife and wild habitats in your area.

Further Reading

Burroughs, John. *John Burroughs' America: Selections from the Writings of the Hudson River Naturalist.* New York: Dover, 1997.

Carson, Rachel. *The Sense of Wonder.* New York: HarperCollins, 1998.

Goodall, Jane. *Forty Years at Gombe.* New York: Stewart, Tabori & Chang, 1999.

Leopold, Aldo. *A Sand County Almanac.* New York: Oxford University Press, 1987.

Morse, Susan C. and Sullivan, Tim J. *Tracks and Signs of North American Carnivores and Other Focal Species.* Huntington, Vt.: Keeping Track, Inc., 2002.

Ryden, Hope. *Bobcat Year.* New York: Viking Press, 1981.

Swinburne, Stephen R. *Bobcat: North America's Cat.* Honesdale, Pa.: Boyds Mills Press, 2001.

———. *Coyote: North America's Dog.* Honesdale, Pa.: Boyds Mills Press, 1999.

———. *Once a Wolf: How Wildlife Biologists Fought to Bring Back the Wolf.* Boston: Houghton Mifflin, 1999.

Wilson, Edward O. *Naturalist.* Washington, D.C.: Island Press, 1994.

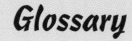

Backtracking—Following the tracks from where the animal has come rather than where it is going.

Biodiversity—The variety of all living things on earth.

Buck—A male deer.

Carnivore—An animal that eats meat.

Cervid—Members of the deer family, including moose, elk, and deer.

Core habitat—Huge areas of wild habitat that provide food, water, shelter, and adequate space to support healthy populations of native species.

Lynx kitten. "If I could come back as an animal, it would be a Canada lynx," says Sue. "I think the lynx embodies the raw, snow-filled, dazzling purity of another time."

Corridors—The linkage zones or land between core habitats that allow animals to come and go.

Cover—Trees, shrubs, rocks, and other natural things in the environment that offer escape, protection, shelter, or denning space to animals.

Ecology—The study of plants and animals in their habitat.

Endangered species—A plant or animal species that is in danger of becoming extinct because of human actions or long-term environmental change.

Generalist—An animal, such as a coyote, that will hunt and eat whatever is available. A generalist may also eat plants and scavenge on dead animals.

Habitat fragmentation—The isolation of plants and animals from other species when development of houses and roads in a large area results in habitat loss.

Habitat productivity—The quality of habitat in terms of its abundance and diversity of food for an animal.

Herbivore—A plant-eater.

Home range—The amount of land needed by a wild animal in order to live, eat, find a mate, and raise young.

Indicator species—Animals that are most vulnerable to habitat disturbance, such as bobcats, river otters, and black bears.

Lactation—The production of milk by a mammal mother for her young.

Olfactory—Relating to the sense of smell in animals.

Ossification—The hardening of antlers into bone.

Rut—Mating season.

Scat—The feces of an animal.

Sign—Any evidence of an animal's presence, including tracks, scats, scrapes, claw marks on trees, antler rub marks on trees, and urine in snow.

Social status—The standing or rank of an animal in a group or herd.

Sow—An adult female bear.

Specialist—An animal that hunts and eats mainly one kind of prey. The main food of the lynx, for example, is the snowshoe hare.

Ungulate—A large, hoofed animal such as a moose, deer, bison, or elk.

Velvet—The soft, blood-engorged tissue covering growing antlers.

Palm trees in Florida show signs of bear—this one is marked with claw scratches.

Index